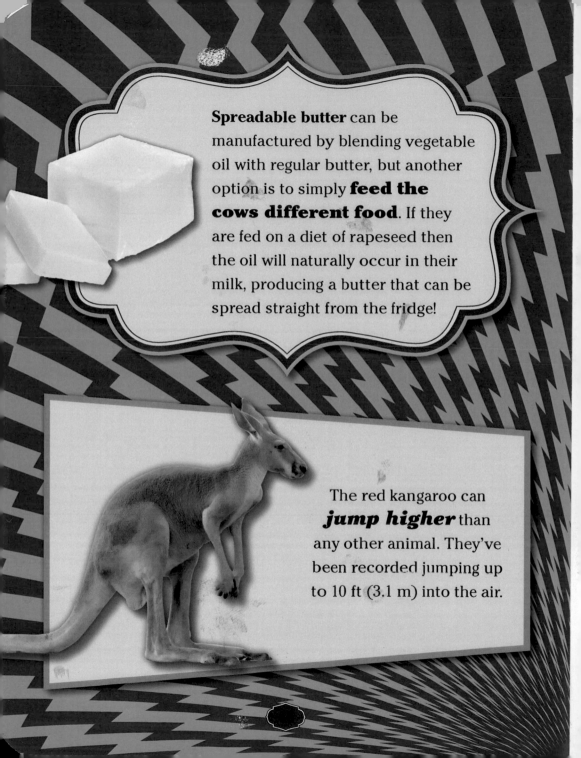

Spreadable butter can be manufactured by blending vegetable oil with regular butter, but another option is to simply **feed the cows different food**. If they are fed on a diet of rapeseed then the oil will naturally occur in their milk, producing a butter that can be spread straight from the fridge!

The red kangaroo can *jump higher* than any other animal. They've been recorded jumping up to 10 ft (3.1 m) into the air.

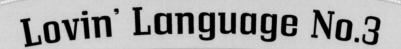

The **longest single-syllable** English word is often claimed to be 'screeched', which is nine letters long. There is indeed no longer word in regular usage, but there are several other valid nine-letter single-syllable words, including 'scratched', 'scrounged', 'stretched', and 'strengths'! Meanwhile, the British *Oxford English Dictionary* also provides the ten-letter 'scraunched', which is an obsolete word meaning 'crunched noisily'.

The only English word starting and ending with a 'z' is **'zizz'**, referring to a buzzing sound, although some dictionaries also allow 'zzz'—a snoring sound.

Worldwide Wonder No.3

There are over *7 billion people alive* on Earth right now, out of around 110 billion who have ever lived. If everyone alive right now stood right next to one another, they'd fit into an area of 1,300 square km (500 square miles).

The capital of Western Australia, Perth, is **closer** to the capital of Indonesia, Jakarta, than it is to Australia's own capital, Canberra.

There is more **fresh water** in the atmosphere than in *all of the rivers on the planet* combined.

Hamsters have a **shorter pregnancy period** than any other placental mammal–just **16 days!** Each litter can contain 20 or more young, and the mother can become pregnant again immediately.

Amazingly, **all pet golden hamsters** are descended from a single brother and sister pairing made in the 1930s. Prior to that, researchers had been unable to breed and domesticate hamsters.